American Gothic,
by Grant Wood, 1930,
oil on beaverboard,
The Art Institute of
Chicago, Friends of the
American Art Collection

THE ART OF AMERICA
IN THE EARLY TWENTIETH CENTURY

By Shirley Glubok
Designed by Gerard Nook

MACMILLAN PUBLISHING CO., INC.
New York
COLLIER MACMILLAN PUBLISHERS
London

The author gratefully acknowledges the kind assistance of:
Mildred Baker, former Associate Curator, The Newark Museum; *Christopher Finch*; *Morrison Heckscher*,
Curator, American Wing, The Metropolitan Museum of Art; *Weston J. Naef*, Assistant Curator,
Department of Prints and Photographs, The Metropolitan Museum of Art; *Lewis Sharp*, Assistant Curator,
American Paintings and Sculpture, The Metropolitan Museum of Art; *Hilary Caws*; *Joel Rosenbaum*;
and especially the helpful cooperation of
Henry Geldzahler, Curator, Twentieth Century Art, The Metropolitan Museum of Art

Other books by Shirley Glubok:

THE ART OF ANCIENT EGYPT
THE ART OF LANDS IN THE BIBLE
THE ART OF ANCIENT GREECE
THE ART OF THE NORTH AMERICAN INDIAN
THE ART OF THE ESKIMO
THE ART OF ANCIENT ROME
THE ART OF AFRICA
ART AND ARCHAEOLOGY
THE ART OF ANCIENT PERU
THE ART OF THE ETRUSCANS
THE ART OF ANCIENT MEXICO
KNIGHTS IN ARMOR
THE ART OF INDIA
THE ART OF JAPAN
HOME AND CHILD LIFE IN COLONIAL DAYS

THE ART OF COLONIAL AMERICA
THE ART OF THE SOUTHWEST INDIANS
THE ART OF THE OLD WEST
THE ART OF THE NEW AMERICAN NATION
THE ART OF THE SPANISH IN THE
    UNITED STATES AND PUERTO RICO
THE ART OF CHINA
THE ART OF AMERICA FROM JACKSON TO LINCOLN
THE ART OF AMERICA IN THE GILDED AGE
THE FALL OF THE AZTECS
THE FALL OF THE INCAS
DISCOVERING TUT-ANKH-AMEN'S TOMB
DISCOVERING THE ROYAL TOMBS AT UR
DIGGING IN ASSYRIA

Front cover illustration: *Children Roller Skating*, by William Glackens,
around 1912, oil, The Brooklyn Museum, Gift of Laura L. Barnes.
Back cover illustration: *After School*, by Raphael Soyer, 1925, oil,
Collection of Mary Soyer Lieber, courtesy of Forum Gallery.

Macmillan Publishing Co., Inc., 866 Third Avenue, New York, N.Y. 10022
Collier-Macmillan Canada Ltd.
Printed in the United States of America

1 2 3 4 5 6 7 8 9 10

Library of Congress Cataloging in Publication Data
Glubok, Shirley.   The art of America in the early twentieth century.
1. Art, American—Juvenile literature. 2. Art, Modern—20th century—United States—Juvenile literature.
[1. Art, American—History. 2. Art, Modern—20th century] I. Title.
N6512.G57   709'.73   74-6329   ISBN 0-02-736180-2 (lib. bdg.)

Backyards, Greenwich Village, by John Sloan, 1914, oil,
Whitney Museum of American Art, New York

When the American people greeted the new twentieth century, quiet farm and village life was giving way to the clatter and bustle of manufacturing and expanding trade and commerce. Rapid transportation and communication quickened the pace of life. Cities grew larger as masses of people came to them from farms and small towns in America and from countries all over the world.

The increasing importance of city life, the growth of industry and the influence of ideas from Europe led American artists to seek new ways of expressing themselves and their times.

Early in the century a group of artists began to record the life of the city. They painted realistic scenes that had long been considered unsuitable subjects for art. William Glackens and John Sloan, who worked as artist-reporters for a newspaper in Philadelphia, developed a method of making rapid sketches to tell a story. They moved to New York City and lived in the Greenwich Village section, where artists from all over America gathered. In the painting by Glackens below, a woman is signaling one of the new electric trolley cars that replaced horse-drawn cars.

The Green Car, 1910, oil, The Metropolitan Museum of Art, Arthur H. Hearn Fund, 1937

Sixth Avenue Elevated at Third Street, 1928, oil, Whitney Museum of American Art

The quick pace of the city is caught in this painting by Sloan of the "El," as the elevated railroad was called, roaring along above a broad street in Greenwich Village.

Sloan and Glackens and six other artists, who became known as "The Eight," exhibited their paintings together at a New York art gallery. Some of the group were referred to as the "Ash Can School" because they painted city slums and back alleys.

Hester Street, 1905, oil, The Brooklyn Museum, Dick S. Ramsay Fund

George Luks had also been an artist-reporter in Philadelphia before moving to New York. In Luks's painting of a street scene on the Lower East Side of New York, children watch a demonstration of a mechanical toy while grownups chat with each other. Thousands of immigrants who came from Europe lived on the Lower East Side.

Maurice Prendergast, of Boston, was the only member of The Eight who did not live in New York, but he often visited there. Prendergast, who painted people at play, flattened and simplified the forms in his pictures by applying his paints in broad strokes of color. In the watercolor below he carefully placed the figures in the playground and the boats on the river to give them equal attention, creating an overall pattern. Prendergast developed his own original style of painting while studying in Europe, where he became aware of new styles in art.

The East River, 1901, pencil and watercolor, The Museum of Modern Art, New York, Gift of Abby Aldrich Rockefeller

The leader of The Eight was Robert Henri, an important art teacher first in Philadelphia and then in New York. Henri painted this portrait of his wife dressed for a party. He worked with swift brush strokes. There is no background to take attention away from Mrs. Henri, who looks as if she is ready to step out of the picture and greet us. Mrs. Henri was herself an artist; she signed her maiden name, Marjorie Organ, to her work.

In the painting at right by Charles Hawthorne, a girl, looking thoughtful and slightly nervous, is standing patiently while a seamstress measures her for a

The Masquerade Dress, 1911, oil,
The Metropolitan Museum of Art,
Arthur H. Hearn Fund, 1958

wedding dress. The seamstress and the girl's mother, who sits busily sewing, seem

to be occupied with their own thoughts.

Hawthorne spent winters in New York but was not as interested in city subjects

as were members of The Eight. He started a summer art school in Provincetown,

Massachusetts, which became an important artists' colony.

The Trousseau, 1910, oil, The Metropolitan Museum of Art,
George A. Hearn Fund, 1911

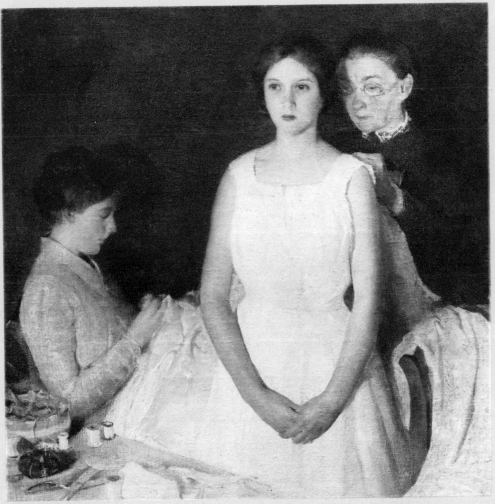

oxing in the ring was a favorite subject of George Bellows, who had himself been a boxer and a professional baseball player. He used rapid, slashing brush strokes to catch the excitement of athletes savagely pounding each other.

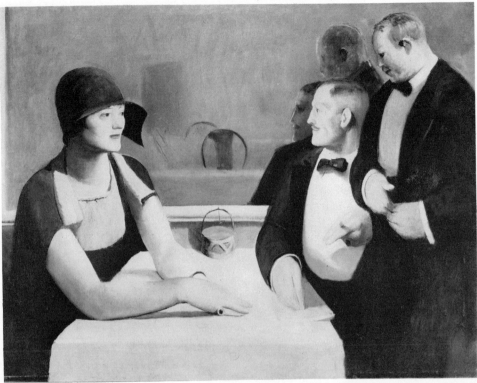

Mr. and Mrs. Chester Dale Dining Out, mid 1920's, oil,
The Metropolitan Museum of Art, Gift of Chester Dale, 1963

Prize fights in public places were illegal; they were allowed only at private clubs. This fight took place at Sharkey's Athletic Club in New York, across the street from Robert Henri's art school, where Bellows studied.

Another of Henri's pupils, Guy Pène duBois, painted a wealthy stockbroker and his wife in a restaurant, which was an unusual setting for a portrait. He simplified the figures, and he repeated the forms of the stockbroker, the waiter and one of the chairs by painting their reflections in the mirror.

1908, oil, The Metropolitan Museum of Art,
Gift of Friends of the Sculptor, 1908

Kenyon Cox chose the New York studio of Augustus Saint-Gaudens as

the setting for his portrait of the sculptor. The painter caught his subject at work

modeling a clay portrait with one hand while clutching a lump of clay and a

sculptor's tool in the other. All of the works of art in the room are by

Saint-Gaudens, except the head of the woman.

Rockwell Kent traveled about the world from Ireland to South America. He sailed on a freighter around Cape Horn and spent a winter on an island in Alaska with his young son. He wrote stories of his travel adventures and illustrated his own books. Kent had a great respect for nature; people are not important in his works. In this lonely scene, painted on Monhegan Island, Maine, the men in the rowboat can hardly be noticed in the frozen landscape.

Winter, 1907, oil, The Metropolitan Museum of Art,
George A. Hearn Fund, 1917

Portrait of Ralph Dusenberry, 1924, oil on canvas with applied wood and paper,
The Metropolitan Museum of Art, The Alfred Stieglitz Collection, 1949

While many American artists were painting what they saw in the real world around them, others were finding new ways of looking at life. In Paris, the art center of the world in the early twentieth century, modern artists were experimenting with ways of expressing themselves that were very different from realistic painting. They felt that a work of art does not need to represent objects that can be recognized. They were making abstract pictures, those in which forms and symbols are the subjects, rather than reproducing the natural appearance of things.

Arthur Dove, who studied in Paris, experimented with the new styles of the French painters. He was the first American to make abstract pictures. Above is Dove's collage portrait of his friend Ralph Dusenberry, in which symbols are used to represent the man's life and character. Dusenberry lived on a boat and swam like a fish, as suggested by the worn wooden shingles. The flag stands for his patriotism; the carpenter's folding ruler framing the picture, for his work in building houses. A piece of a printed song sheet shows the words of a hymn he often sang. The collage method of gluing wood and paper onto a painting was used by modern artists in France.

When Joseph Stella returned from study in Italy and France, he was startled by the glaring new world that was being created by steel and electricity. The speed of modern life was expressed in his abstract painting of the Brooklyn Bridge. The curving lines swinging upward represent the steel cables of the bridge. The rectangular shapes within the arches suggest the towering skyscrapers of the city. The oval shapes are electric lights. Making movement the subject of a painting is an idea that came from a group of abstract painters in Europe known as "futurists."

The Bridge, 1922, gouache, The Newark Museum

The Rope Dancer Accompanies Herself With Her Shadows

1916, oil, The Museum of Modern Art, Gift of G. David Thompson

One of the most advanced experimental painters and photographers of the early twentieth century gave up his real name when he was still in school and adopted the name Man Ray. Like many other modern artists, Man Ray painted what he saw in his imagination, rather than the natural appearance of objects. He used broad shapes and flattened forms to illustrate what he called *The Rope Dancer Accompanies Herself with Her Shadows*, above.

Alfred Stieglitz, one of America's great photographers, had an art gallery at 291 Fifth Avenue in New York. "291," as it came to be called, was the first gallery in America to show the paintings of European moderns such as Paul Cézanne, Henri Matisse and Pablo Picasso. Stieglitz was also interested in American painters who were going in new directions. He exhibited the work of the artist Georgia O'Keeffe, whom he later married.

O'Keeffe represented the huge skyscrapers rapidly rising in New York in her painting of the American Radiator Building. Stieglitz's name appears at the left of the building. O'Keeffe now lives in New Mexico, where she paints her personal view of the mountains and desert.

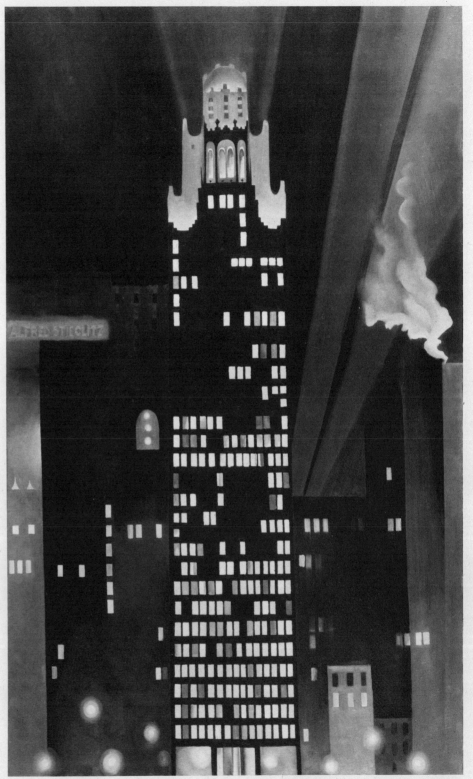

1927, oil, Fiske Art Museum, Nashville, Tennessee

1915–1916, oil on board, Philadelphia Museum of Art,
The Alfred Stieglitz Collection

Marsden Hartley lived for a time in Taos, New Mexico, where a number of American artists had gathered. The colorful *santos,* or holy images, of the Spanish settlers appealed to Hartley. In *Blessing of the Melon* at left, he omitted all details and simplified the painting into a pattern of circles, ovals, loops, stripes, stars, triangles and rectangles.

John Marin, who spent his summers on the coast of Maine, simplified his seascapes of boats, waves and rocky shores. Day after day he went out on the water looking for interesting views. Working swiftly in watercolor, he caught the movement of the choppy sea and the dipping sailboats and pounding waves. Marin used triangles and rectangles to represent waves, rocks, buildings and even clouds. But his paintings are never completely abstract; he always included some objects that can be recognized.

Pertaining to Stonington Harbor, Maine, No. 4, 1926, watercolor, The Metropolitan Museum of Art, The Alfred Stieglitz Collection, 1949

1915, oil, The Metropolitan Museum of Art, George A. Hearn Fund, 1967

Max Weber, the son of a Russian tailor, was ten years old when his family moved to New York. Later he studied in Paris, where he became interested in the "cubists," a group of experimental artists. Instead of painting the natural shapes of objects, the cubists represented them with cylinders, cubes, pyramids and cones. In *Athletic Contest* Weber used the cubist method of opening objects and flattening them so that the same object could be seen from several points of view. The repetition of figures of athletes in action and of numbers and symbols increases the excitement of the event.

Stuart Davis also expressed the energetic pace of American life in abstract styles. In *New York Waterfront* smokestacks, ventilators, steam pipes and buildings can be identified. Other forms are reduced to flat shapes and arranged in a pattern of the artist's invention. The letters L R C add to the puzzle-like quality of the painting.

Davis was one of many American artists who exhibited their paintings in an international art show held in an armory in New York in 1913. The Armory Show included the latest works of the French painters Paul Gauguin and Marcel Duchamp and the Dutch artist Vincent Van Gogh. For the first time, the American general public became aware of European developments in art. Most people had never seen abstract art before and they were shocked. It took years for the American public to accept modern art and take it seriously.

1938, gouache, The Museum of Modern Art

A group of artists known as "precisionists" were inspired by the structure of the machines and tall buildings of the modern world. They painted with hard edges and straight lines. Charles Sheeler, who found subjects in the country's rapidly growing industries, often painted and photographed machinery. In *Upper Deck* electric motors and exhaust fans on a large ship become beautiful, clear forms.

The title of *I Saw the Figure Five in Gold*, by Charles Demuth, was taken from a poem by William Carlos Williams. The figure 5 was on a fire truck that sped through the dark city at night. In the painting a 5 covers almost the entire area and is repeated in smaller forms to indicate that the wheels of the fire truck are rolling rapidly away from us. The rectangular shapes represent walls of buildings. The round bulbs on the tips of the 5's repeat the pattern of the circular street lights. The chopped-off signs add to the feeling of speed.

1929, oil, Fogg Art Museum, Harvard University,
Louise E. Bettens Fund

1928, oil on composition board,
The Metropolitan Museum of Art,
The Alfred Stieglitz Collection, 1949

While some American artists were working in the latest European styles, others were painting American scenes in a more traditional manner. In this view of the coast of Maine by Edward Hopper, the artist was interested in the pattern of light and shadows on the tower and the lighthouse keeper's house beside it. The buildings are crisply outlined against the sky. They seem to rise directly from the earth, with no trees in front of them to distract from their flat surfaces. Because of the severe New England winters a passageway connects the lighthouse and the dwellings beside it.

There is a sense of loneliness in Hopper's pictures. Even when he painted people, there is a feeling that they are isolated, apart from the rest of the world.

The Lighthouse at Two Lights, 1929, oil, The Metropolitan Museum of Art, Hugo Kastor Fund, 1962

25

1918, watercolor and gouache, The Museum of Modern Art,
Gift of A. Conger Goodyear

Charles Burchfield, who grew up in Ohio, lived briefly in New York but was not

interested in the developments of the new modern art movement. He preferred to

live in Ohio and to portray his memories—the joys and fears of his own childhood.

Burchfield expressed the sounds and moods of nature in his fresh and original paintings.

In the dreamlike *The Night Wind* at left, the clouds and wind seem to come to life and the windows of the house look like large round eyes.

Walt Disney created his world of make-believe through animated motion pictures in which trees and flowers move and talk and animals act like people. Disney invented the character Mickey Mouse, who was the hero of many cartoons. In the scene below from *Mickey's Choo Choo*, the Disney hero is driving a locomotive with a human face.

To make an animated cartoon, each little change in position of the characters has to be painted separately. A series of pictures showing every slight movement is then photographed in sequence against the same background. When projected onto a screen in rapid succession, the sequence makes the characters seem animated, or moving.

1929, ink on celluloid and paper, © Walt Disney Productions

Twenty Cent Movie, 1936, egg tempera on composition board,
Whitney Museum of American Art

As talking pictures replaced silent films, motion pictures became increasingly

popular and people flocked to movies for entertainment. Reginald Marsh painted this

lively street scene in front of a movie theater. Posters of film stars and advertisements of movies form an interesting background to the moviegoers dressed in typical 1930's fashions. Marsh, who had been a newspaper and magazine illustrator, loved to walk the streets of New York and watch the people. He was one of the post-World-War-I realists whose interest had shifted away from the European manner of painting.

Isabel Bishop also paints commonplace events, concentrating on working girls in the city. Her subjects never look posed. In *Two Girls*, below, one young woman reads a letter while the other watches her intently. There is very little background in the picture, only a teacup in the corner and the hint of a chair to suggest that the scene is indoors.

1936, oil and tempera on presswood, The Metropolitan Museum of Art,
Arthur H. Hearn Fund, 1936, courtesy of Midtown Galleries

The Great Depression of the 1930's was a very difficult time for people in America. In 1935, during President Franklin D. Roosevelt's administration, Congress voted funds to set up the Works Progress Administration, known as the WPA, to relieve unemployment. Under the WPA the Federal Art Project was developed to give jobs to thousands of artists throughout the country. Painting murals on the walls of public buildings was one of its programs.

The Federal Art Project not only helped artists to survive this desperate period, it also brought their work before the general public. Philip Evergood and Ben Shahn both participated in it. Like many other artists working during the Depression, they felt that art should be used to make the world a better place to live in.

A little girl feeding bread to birds from an apartment window is

1939, oil on composition board, Whitney Museum of American Art

the subject of *Lily and the Sparrows* by Philip Evergood. Perhaps she has no place to play outdoors and the only birds she sees are those at her window.

Shahn, who immigrated to America from Lithuania, painted this scene to show the world something he thought was unjust. In 1927 a poor shoemaker, Nicola Sacco, and a fish peddler, Bartolomeo Vanzetti, had been electrocuted for a murder which they were accused of committing. People all over the world heard about it and many thought the trial was unfair and that the men were innocent. Shahn emphasizes the importance of the scene by showing only the simplified forms of the dead men and the judges and lawyers who participated in the trial.

The Passion of Sacco and Vanzetti, 1931–1932,
tempera on canvas, Whitney Museum of American Art,
Gift of Mr. and Mrs. Milton Lowenthal in memory of Juliana Force

Another artist who participated in the Federal Art Project, Grant Wood, was born on a farm in Iowa, and after studying in Europe he returned to Iowa to live. Wood was one of a group of artists known as "regionalists," who painted the Midwestern life they knew with freshness, as if they had just discovered it. Wood made complete sketches for his pictures, then worked slowly, applying many layers of paint.

Dinner for Threshers is a long view of the interior of a farmhouse. The men have come in from the fields for their noonday meal, which was prepared by the women on the wood-burning stove. A hand pump beside the stove brings water in from a well.

On the porch, one farmer is washing his face and another combs his hair, while a boy brings a bucketful of water from an outside pump.

The picture is fascinating as a record of nineteenth-century farm traditions that lasted into the 1930's in some areas. Every detail of the house, including the screen door and kerosene lamp, the farmers, the women and even the farmyard, is very carefully painted. The artist liked to copy painted decorations from chinaware. His interest in these patterns can be seen in the wallpaper, the women's dresses, the men's shirts, the curtains, the tablecloth and even the china cupboard.

1934, tempera on panel, Private Collection, New York, courtesy of Wildenstein & Co.

The Tornado, 1929, oil, The Hackley Art Gallery, Muskegon, Michigan

Deadly tornadoes frequently strike in some sections of the Midwest. John Steuart Curry, who liked to paint scenes of man's struggle with the forces of nature, showed a tense moment before a storm broke in Kansas. The cone shape of the tornado can be seen in the distance as the farmer and his family hurry to the storm cellar. The mother clutches her baby, the children grab their pets; even the dog runs after her puppies as the farmer urges them all to safety.

Thomas Hart Benton, who, like Curry, Wood and Burchfield, is considered a "regionalist," is the son of a Missouri congressman. He painted murals for the Truman Memorial Library in Independence, Missouri, and the Missouri State Capitol. In both his murals and his smaller works, he records rural Americans at work. The scene at right shows a boy picking corn on a Missouri farm. Benton's figures seem taller and thinner than they are in real life.

Roasting Ears, 1938–1939, egg tempera with oil glazes,
The Metropolitan Museum of Art, Arthur H. Hearn Fund, 1939

35

American sculptors were slower than painters in breaking away from the realistic tradition of earlier American art. When a statue of America's sixteenth president was made for the Lincoln Memorial in Washington, D.C., it was carved in the realistic manner from 170 tons of Georgia marble. The sculptor, Daniel Chester French, first modeled a small sketch less than three feet high out of clay. From this he made an eight-foot plaster model, slightly changing the pose and making the details sharper. The final statue was carved out of twenty-eight blocks of marble by the Piccirilli brothers, a family of New York stoneworkers. Many sculptors of the period, however, disapproved of having other stonecutters work on their statues. These "direct carvers" preferred to sculpt their own figures from start to finish.

Paul Manship was one of the first American sculptors to experiment with modern methods. Manship simplified the forms of his statues, rather than showing all of the details of their bodies. This bronze dancer and her gazelles are sleek and graceful. The curves of the flowing drapery create the rhythmic balance of the group.

1916, The Metropolitan Museum of Art,
Lathrop Fund, 1959

The sculptor Elie Nadelman collected antique dolls and toys, and his own statues are often playful. The surfaces of his figures are sleek curves with all details eliminated, leaving only the rounded forms. His bronze *Man in the Open Air* has a full body dwindling to delicate ankles and tiny feet and hands. The man's bow tie and his derby hat stand out on the smooth form.

Funny little wire figures, created for his own amusement, led Alexander Calder to an original sculptural style. Calder, whose father and grandfather were also sculptors, had studied to be an engineer, but then went to Paris to be in the center of the art world. Calder's little wire figures led

About 1915,
The Museum of Modern Art,
Gift of William S. Paley

1929, wire,
The Museum of Modern Art,
Gift of Edward M. M. Warburg

Lobster Trap and Fish Tail, 1939, painted steel wire and
sheet aluminum, The Museum of Modern Art, Commissioned by
the Advisory Committee for the stairwell of the Museum

to experiments with wire forms suspended in space, then to his development of

the mobile. Weights and counterweights of various forms and shapes are hung at the

ends of long, curving wires that stretch out in many directions. The slightest touch

or current of air will set them dancing in motion.

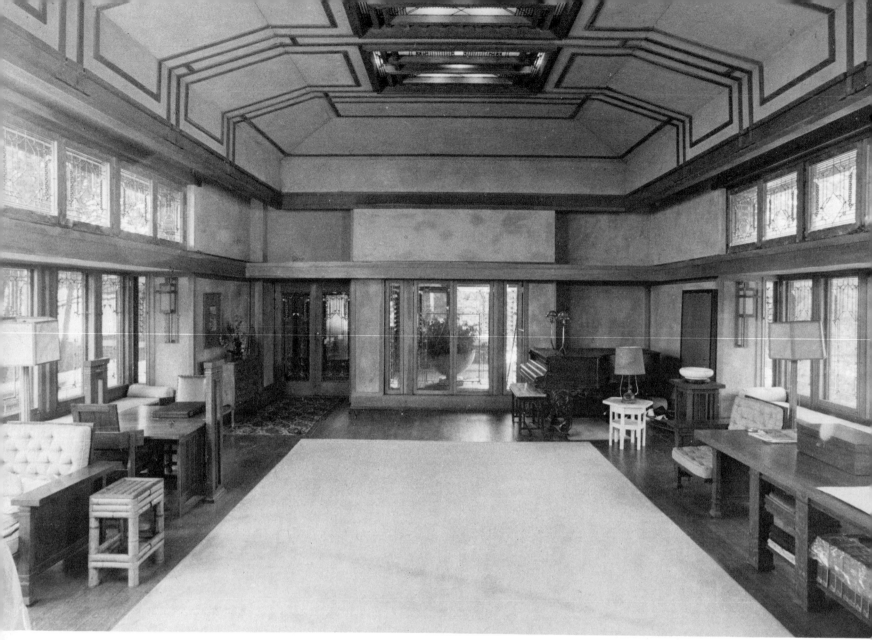

1912–1915, The Metropolitan Museum of Art,
Purchase: Bequest of Emily C. Chadbourne, 1972

The foremost American architect in the early twentieth century was Frank Lloyd

Wright. He is known for his "Prairie School" style, so called because it is designed to fit

the flat landscape of the Midwest. "Prairie Houses" are long and low, without attics or

basements. Wright liked to build his houses of natural, native materials, and he built them for comfort, convenience and efficiency. In order to give the interiors a sense of flowing space, he often designed the whole lower floor as one room.

The living room of Northome, in Minnesota, has large windows to provide a long view of the lake that the house overlooked. The windows are set with patterns of stained, or colored, glass divided by strips of lead. The architect designed the table and armchairs in the room, which can be seen here in closer view.

Wright liked to design the furniture for his houses so that it would relate to the architecture. His furniture is square-shaped, blending with the straight lines of the rooms. There is no fancy carving to detract from the clean lines and the natural color and texture of the wood itself.

1902

1902

1936, photograph by Hedrich-Blessing

Frank Lloyd Wright's most famous house, built about thirty years after Northome, is Falling Water, at Bear Run, Pennsylvania. The architect felt that homes should fit in with their natural setting. Falling Water was built over a mountain stream.

The cantilevers extending over the cliff are constructed of reinforced concrete and anchored into the rocky walls of the mountain. These terraces hanging over the stream give the house a light, floating quality. The main part of the house has walls of rough stone, with large panes of glass for views of nature.

The skyscraper, developed by American architects in Chicago in the late nineteenth century, is the architectural symbol of America. The wealth, power and scientific achievement of the country made skyscrapers possible. As the twentieth century progressed, office buildings stretched taller and taller. For about forty years New York's Empire State Building, 103 stories high, was the tallest skyscraper in the world. Sixty thousand tons of steel were used for the skeleton of the building.

The Empire State Building rests on the solid bedrock of the earth, which is close to the surface in New York City and gives a firm foundation to the high buildings of Manhattan. This photograph was taken in 1931, shortly after the Empire State Building was erected. The mast for mooring dirigibles, large balloon-shaped airships that were then a modern form of transportation, can be seen on top. Today a television antenna sits on top of the mooring mast.

Architects Shreve, Lamb and Harmon,
1930–1931, Wurts-Photo 1931

The idea that a photograph can be a work of art was established in America largely through the efforts of Alfred Stieglitz. He was the leader of the "Photo-Secessionists," a group of camera artists who exhibited at the 291 Gallery. He also published a magazine called *Camera Work* that reproduced works by some of the most talented photographers of the day. Below is Stieglitz's picture of the Staten Island Ferry. The ferry boat, bathed in dim light, seems to be emerging from a mist as it nears the dock. Crowds of people have pushed to the forward deck, impatient to get off.

Stieglitz explored New York with a little hand camera. He called it his "detective camera" because it was small compared to other cameras of the day, even though it made plates four by five inches in size. Sometimes he took many exposures from the same spot. Often he would stand for hours, even in the snow or rain, waiting for the moment when the

1911, The Metropolitan Museum of Art

light was right and his subjects were in just the right position, before snapping the shutter.

In California Edward Weston was leader of a group of photographers called "f/64," named after the smallest aperture, or opening, in a camera lens shutter. Weston worked with a camera that used film eight by ten inches in size, and made his prints from the full negative.

At the San Francisco World's Fair in 1915, Weston saw modern abstract painting for the first time. In the late 1920's he began to experiment with his own photographic vision, taking extremely close-up views of everyday objects such as sea shells, cabbages and driftwood. Their shapes and textures became the focus of his attention. Weston's *Green Pepper* glows in the velvety light, its smooth form looking like a piece of sculpture rather than a vegetable.

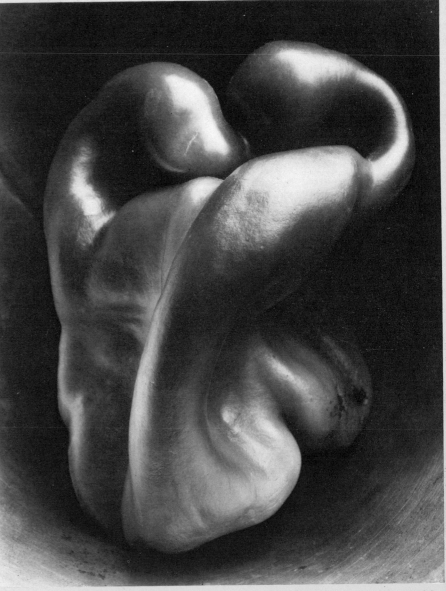

1930, The Metropolitan Museum of Art,
David Hunter McAlpin Fund, 1957

Westchester, New York, Farmhouse, 1931,
Philadelphia Museum of Art,
The Art Sales and Rental Gallery Fund

Outdoor rural scenes in full sunlight were often photographed by Walker

Evans. His picture of a farmhouse in New York State is carefully composed.

Although no people are in sight, the house seems to be occupied, as if someone

will step out any moment and start the car.

During the Depression Evans traveled around the country photographing for the Farm Security Administration, or FSA, set up by the government to help relocate farmers who had lost their land. Because of drought and dust storms, thousands of farms were not producing crops, and farmers lost ownership of their land because they could not pay their debts.

The FSA sent photographers into rural areas to record the lives of jobless farm workers. They wanted unposed pictures of rural poverty to publish in newspapers and magazines to make the public aware of the unfortunate conditions. Dorothea Lange, working for the FSA, photographed a migrant farm mother with her children. In spite of her worry, the woman looks proud and strong.

Migrant Mother, Nipomo, California, 1936, Library of Congress

Tables for Ladies, by Edward Hopper, 1930, oil,
The Metropolitan Museum of Art, George A. Hearn Fund, 1931

Life in America went through a series of major changes during the first four decades of the twentieth century. The early growth of industry exploded into the First World War. The excitement of the twenties crashed into the despair of the Depression. By the end of the period the world was on the brink of another war.

American art could not reflect so much variety in a single style. It became many styles, some related, some totally at odds with the others. By the end of the 1930's American art had become truly modern and had joined the mainstream of international art. New York City had become the art center of the world.